CULTURE IN ACTION

Preening, Painting, and Piercing
Body Art

John Bliss

Raintree is an imprint of Capstone Global Library Limited,
a company incorporated in England and Wales having its
registered office at 7 Pilgrim Street, London, EC4V 6LB
– Registered company number: 6695582

Text © Capstone Global Library Limited 2011
First published in hardback in 2011
The moral rights of the proprietor have been asserted.

Edited by Louise Galpine, Megan Cotugno, and Abby Colich
Designed by Ryan Frieson
Original illustrations © Capstone Global Library Ltd
Illustrated by Cavedweller Studio, Randy Schirz
Picture research by Liz Alexander
Originated by Capstone Global Library Ltd
Printed in China by China Translation & Printing
Services Ltd

ISBN 978 1 40621 717 9
15 14 13 12 11 10
10 9 8 7 6 5 4 3 2 1

British Library Cataloguing in Publication Data
Bliss, John
Preening, painting, and piercing: Body art. – (Culture in
action)
391.6-dc22
A full catalogue record for this book is available from the
British Library.

Acknowledgements
We would like to thank the following for permission to
reproduce photographs: Courtesy of The Advertising Archives
p. **10**; Alamy pp. **4** (© Deco), **5** (© lemonlight features), **6**
(© Mary Evans Picture Library), **9** (© imagebroker), **24**
(© Pictorial Press Ltd), **25** (© F1online digitale Bildagentur
GmbH), **27** (© Mihaela Ninic), **28** (© Mira); Corbis pp. **8**
(© The Gallery Collection), **11** (© Wael Hamzeh/epa), **14**
(© Hans Georg Roth), **22** (© Marco Cauz), **23** (© Diego
Azubel/epa); Getty Images pp. **7** (Sean Gallup), **12** (The
Bridgeman Art Library/French School), **15** (William Thomas
Cain), **26** (Scott Olson); Shutterstock pp. **16** (© gmwnz), **17**
(© Dallas Events Inc), **18** (© Diane Gonzales), **20** (© Knud
Nielsen).

Cover photograph of woman's hands and feet painted with
henna reproduced with permission of Photolibrary (Vivek
Sharma/Asia Images).

We would like to thank Jackie Murphy for her invaluable help
in the preparation of this book.

Every effort has been made to contact copyright holders of
material reproduced in this book. Any omissions will be
rectified in subsequent printings if notice is given to the
publisher.

Disclaimer
All the Internet addresses (URLs) given in this book were valid
at the time of going to press. However, due to the dynamic
nature of the Internet, some addresses may have changed, or
sites may have changed or ceased to exist since publication.
While the author and publisher regret any inconvenience this
may cause readers, no responsibility for any such changes can
be accepted by either the author or the publisher.

Author
John Bliss is a writer and teacher who teaches courses
in Theatre and Communication.

Literacy consultant
Jackie Murphy is Director of Arts at a centre of teaching
and learning. She works with teachers, artists, and
school leaders internationally.

Contents

Important note:

Tattooing and piercing can be very dangerous. They should only be done by people who are trained to perform them safely. NEVER get a tattoo or piercing without permission from your parent or guardian.

Some words are printed in bold, **like this**. You can find out what they mean by looking in the glossary on page 30.

Many kinds of body art

People around the world love to show off. They may do this through the clothes they wear or how they cut their hair.

Many people also decorate their bodies. For example, they may get a **tattoo** or have their ears **pierced**. These decorations are usually **permanent**, which means they last forever. Other kinds of body art, such as make-up and body paint, can be washed away. The ways people decorate their bodies, and the reasons they do so, have changed over the years. But almost every **culture** practises some kind of body art.

This native warrior from Papua New Guinea paints his face before going into battle. The paint is meant to frighten his enemy.

Why do people do it?

People decorate their bodies for many reasons. Some people do it as part of a **ceremony**, or special event. Others want to feel more beautiful. Sometimes it is a way to show something about people's personality.

Some people decorate their bodies in different ways for different reasons. For example, a woman might have a tattoo to show that she is a member of a group, but wear make-up to feel more attractive.

This man and woman show their personalities through many types of body art. They have piercings, tattoos, and have even coloured and sculpted their hair.

The oldest tattoos?

In 1991 climbers found the body of a man frozen in the ice of the Alps. He was more than 5,000 years old. The man had 57 tattoos, which were made out of **soot** from a fire. Many of the tattoos were placed near joints such as the knee and ankle, where people suffer from a pain called arthritis. Because of this, scientists think these tattoos may have been meant to heal pain.

Centuries of body decoration

Body art has always been an important part of people's lives. Humans have painted, **tattooed**, and **pierced** their bodies throughout recorded history – and even before!

Ancient body painting and tattoos

Body paint and tattoos go back to the earliest recorded **cultures**. For example, scientists studying ancient humans in Africa found body paint they think is 400,000 years old. A 2,500-year-old mummy (preserved body) found in China has animal tattoos on his arm, shoulder, and back. In 54 BC, the Roman emperor Julius Caesar wrote about painted and tattooed **tribes** he saw living in northern Europe.

The Picts lived in Scotland during the time of the Roman Empire. Their name means "painted people".

Egypt, Greece, and Rome

About 4,000 years ago, Egyptian men and women shaved unwanted hair. Body oils were part of the wages paid to workers. Egyptians wore eye make-up and women coloured their lips.

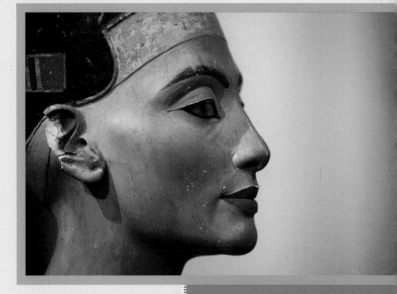

Nefertiti was the queen of Egypt around 1350 BC. Notice the use of eye make-up on this statue of her.

The ancient Greeks and Romans also experimented with body decoration. Around 500 BC, Greek women used white lead (a kind of metal) to make their skin appear lighter. (Since then, we have learned that lead can be poisonous.) Eye shadow and **blusher** were also popular. Greek and Roman women dyed their hair and wore wigs. About 2,000 years ago, Roman women used products to make their skin soft, including one made from crocodile **dung** (solid waste).

Iranian beauty queen

In 2006 scientists working in Iran discovered women's items that were 5,000 years old. Among these items were a box for make-up, a comb, and a bowl and marble tool used for applying eyeliner.

A rebirth of body art

During the 1400s and 1500s, European explorers travelled to many distant places. The Italian explorer Christopher Columbus sailed to the Americas in 1492, and the English explorer Sir Francis Drake circled the globe from 1577 to 1580. Everywhere these explorers went, they discovered painted, tattooed, and pierced people. They brought new ideas about body art home with them.

Pale faces

Make-up became popular in Europe in the 1500s. Farmers and labourers had dark and rough skin from working in the sun. As a result queens – and kings – lightened their faces with pale paint and powder. This showed they were rich and that did not have to work outdoors. It also made them seem young and healthy.

Soon the upper classes started following this example. But the lower classes did not have time or money to spend on make-up.

In the 1500s, Queen Elizabeth I painted her skin white to create an image of purity. Her make-up became known as the "Mask of Youth".

Inked men

In the late 1700s, the explorer Captain James Cook made three voyages to the islands of the South Pacific. He described the tattooed people he saw and even brought one man back to England. Many of Cook's men, including his science officer, got tattooed. Over the next 100 years, tattooing spread throughout Europe.

This **Maori** chief lived around 1900. The tattoo on his face is called a **moko**.

Glamour shots

The growth of photography in the late 1800s helped popularize make-up. Women who refused to wear make-up in public would still lighten their skin and colour their eyes, lips, and cheeks for photographs.

The magic of make-up and hair

Make-up has come a long way since the lead paint and crocodile **dung** of the past. Today companies make billions of pounds from selling make-up. Make-up is worn by everyone from film stars to people in your own family.

Make-up can be used both to hide flaws and to highlight facial features. Women, and sometimes men, use make-up to smooth out their skin, call attention to their lips and eyes, and colour their fingernails and toenails.

Make-up products

Common make-up products include foundation, **blusher**, lipstick, and eye make-up such as eyeliner, eye shadow, and mascara. Foundation is used to smooth out the skin. Blusher is used to colour and highlight the cheeks, while lipstick colours the lips. Lipstick in a tube, which is most common today, first appeared in 1915.

FOR THAT S-M-O-O-T-H *Young* LOOK!

★ Add new, thrilling glamour to your looks right now . . . in just a few seconds . . . with "Pan-Cake" make-up, the famous glamorizing make-up originated by *Max Factor Hollywood*. You'll love the smooth, flawless, beautiful new complexion it creates for you . . . and you'll be delighted with the way it helps hide tiny skin faults. Try "Pan-Cake" make-up just once and you'll immediately discover why screen stars say that it is the greatest glamour make-up in the history of cosmetics.

ELLEN DREW
Starring in COLUMBIA'S "THE SWORDSMAN"

PAN-CAKE BRAND MAKE-UP

MAX FACTOR 'Cosmetics of the Stars' are obtainable from your local Chemist, Hairdresser & Store

Complete Your Make-up in Colour Harmony with *Max Factor Hollywood* Face Powder, Rouge and Lipstick.

Max Factor HOLLYWOOD

Polish-American make-up artist Max Factor designed make-up for many Hollywood stars. They then appeared in ads selling his products.

Versions of foundation, blusher, lipstick, and eye make-up have been around since the time of ancient Egypt, but mascara is modern make-up. It is used to colour and thicken eyelashes. Its name came from the Italian word *maschera*, which means "mask". It was first sold in 1913.

Birth of fake lashes

US film director D. W. Griffith invented false eyelashes in 1916. He was directing a film and wanted his actress to have longer lashes. He had a wig maker attach human hair to pieces of thin fabric and then glue them to the actresses' eyelids.

Fashion and make-up go together. This model's make-up highlights her clothing.

Hair-raising hair

Hair and make-up have always gone together. People dye their hair both natural and unusual colours. They may add length or body by adding hairpieces called extensions. Sometimes an entire head is covered with a wig.

Complex hairstyles reached their peak in France in the late 1700s. Hairdressers wove women's hair into wire frames that were sometimes 0.5 to 1 metre (2 to 3 feet) tall. Then they added fake hair, which they held in place with perfumed animal fat. Once the fat dried, the hair was cut into shapes and decorated with beads, fruit, and even live birds.

Since these styles were so expensive to have done, women kept them in place for weeks. By the end of that time, they smelled terrible and sometimes hid spiders – or worse. This might be why we say messy hair is like a rat's nest.

The French queen Marie Antoinette (1755–1793) was known for her creative hairstyles.

Sing its praises

Advertising is an important part of selling beauty products. An important part of advertising is a catchy jingle, or song. Now it is your turn to write a jingle.

Steps to follow:

1. Come up with a product you want to sell. It could be something you have read about in this book, or something you make up, such as Marie Antoinette's Hair Bug Spray. Choose a product you find interesting or gross!

2. Come up with a tune. The easiest way is to use a popular tune or a children's song. For example, "Twinkle, Twinkle, Little Star" is simple and easy to remember.

3. Now decide on the words. What do you want to say about the product? Write down words that rhyme. For "hair" you might write, "air, fair, lair", and so on. Write down words that describe the product. For "bug spray" you might write, "spider, kill, bomb, dead".

4. Put it all together. If you wrote a jingle for hair bug spray using "Twinkle, Twinkle", you might write this:

Marie's Bug Spray for your hair
Kills the spiders if you dare.

Share your jingles. See who has the catchiest tune – or the funniest lyrics!

Have fun sharing your jingles. Use your face and body to help sell your product.

Marie's Bug Spray for your hair Kills the spiders if you dare.

Kathakali is a kind of dance-drama from India. The colours of the make-up have meaning. Green is used for noble characters, while evil characters have red faces and a red beard.

Stage make-up

Stage make-up is much darker than normal make-up, to help performers' faces stand out under the bright stage lights. Actors use make-up to shape their face. They highlight areas they want to stand out and shadow areas they want to make appear deeper. They can create wrinkles and jowls (loose skin), making a young actor appear much older.

In Asian countries such as China, India, and Japan, performers paint themselves in bright colours that are not realistic. In **Kabuki**, a Japanese form of musical drama, human characters have pure-white faces. Other colours show the characters' age, gender, and mood. Characters with pink lines on their face are young and happy, while characters painted deep blue are gloomy.

Am I blue?

The Blue Man Group is a stage show that combines music, comedy, and media such as video. The three performers wear black costumes and blue make-up that covers their entire faces and heads. In this show, make-up is used to make the actors all look alike, rather than different.

From stage to home

Stage make-up helped spark an interest in make-up among the public. In 1911 the Ballets Russes, a famous Russian ballet company, performed in London. The dancers wore striking make-up, especially make-up that highlighted their eyes. Sales of eyeliner and coloured eye shadow then exploded, as women tried to copy the dancers' make-up.

The individual performers of the Blue Man Group disappear beneath their make-up.

Body painting

Body painting is different from make-up. While people wear make-up to appear more beautiful or to play a part, body paint has deeper meanings.

Transformation

Tribal people often paint their bodies as part of a **ceremony**, such as initiations (ceremonies where people join a group), weddings, and funerals. The paint transforms, or changes, the person from an individual to something more, such as a member of a group or a married woman. Body paint is also seen as a kind of protection, which is why some warriors wear it going into battle.

Scientists have found red and black body paints made from minerals, such as iron, that are 75,000 years old. Tribal people today make their paint from seeds, fruits, or coloured clay. The pigment, or colour, is then mixed with oil or animal fat.

This Aboriginal man plays an instrument called a digeridoo while wearing body paint.

Team spirit

Some fans at sporting events paint their faces and bodies in the colours of their favourite team. They feel like tribal warriors!

Temporary tattoos

Body paint is used to create **temporary** (not lasting) tattoos, which are a safe alternative to real tattoos. **Mehndi** is a popular form of temporary tattooing from India. In mehndi, a reddish-brown dye called henna is applied to the skin using a paintbrush or a tool called a stylus. Mehndi tattoos are usually very complex.

Mehndi tattoos are traditionally used as part of wedding ceremonies in India. The dye can last from a week to several months.

Colourful designs are part of face painting. Animals, flowers, and butterflies are always popular designs.

Face painting

Like body painting, face painting often has meaning beyond decoration. Native Americans painted their faces to give them more power in battle or while hunting. They believed the paint would help them draw power from the world around them. Different colours had special meanings. For example, they wore green paint under their eyes to give them better vision at night.

Ancient and modern soldiers paint their face for **camouflage**. They use the colours of the surrounding environment, such as green and brown, to make themselves difficult to see. Hunters sometimes use camouflage, too.

Today, face painting is popular with children and adults at fairs and festivals. Artists use special paints to draw pictures directly onto people's faces. This face painting is just for fun.

Paint your face!

Face painting can be a fun activity. Make sure that you only use face paints provided by an adult.

Steps to follow:

1. First, choose a design. You can find ideas in books and comics, or search for ideas online. Animals, clowns, and superheroes are popular. Keep your first design simple.

2. Use a computer printout or a photocopy of a face to plan your ideas. Try designs that follow the shape of the face. Repeating patterns, like tiger stripes or leopard spots, can be fun. Keep drawing until you get a design you like.

3. Assemble your supplies. Sponges are used to apply paint to a large area. Brushes are used for detailed work.

4. It is time to paint! Painting someone else's face is easier than painting your own, so you might want to do this with a friend or in a group.

You and your friends can paint your faces as part of a group project. For example, you might all be different animals in a zoo.

Don't worry if your painting isn't perfect. As long as it's colourful, no one will know.

Body painting as fine art

Some artists have turned body painting into a fine art, meaning they explore it simply for the sake of beauty. Instead of painting on a canvas, they paint their work directly onto a human model.

The painting may cover one part of a model's body, or it may cover the entire body. Some artists paint the model's body so that he or she disappears into the background. This is an extreme kind of camouflage!

Living statues

In big cities, performers work as "living statues". They paint their bodies to look like stone or metal and wear a costume that is the same colour. Part of the fun is surprising passers-by, who do not know they are actually people. Living statues are also popular at parties.

Though this looks like a statue, it is actually a person painted to look like one. People on the street do not know the person is alive until he moves!

Make a human artwork

Living statues turn their bodies into a piece of art. You and your friends can use your bodies and voices to create a living artwork called a "human machine". When you build your machine, think about the moving parts in factory machines and amusement fairground rides.

Steps to follow:

1. One person repeats a motion and a sound that goes with it. For example, you might move your arms up and down, making a different sound for each movement. Don't think too much about it – just have fun!

2. Now another person joins in with a different movement and sound. This person should build on the movement of the first person. For example, the second person might bend down when the first person pushes his or her arms down.

3. One by one, have other friends join in. Each new person should try to connect with one or more part of the "machine".

4. What is your machine's name? Be creative! What you can make is only limited by your imagination.

Get other people to watch your machine. Ask them what they think it does!

As more people become part of the machine, it becomes more fun. Try to all move together, just like a real machine.

Tattooing

Tattoos are designs or pictures that are **permanently** inked into the skin. People around the world wear tattoos. The various **tribes** Captain Cook met (see page 9) wore tattoos on their faces. Today it is more common for people to get tattoos on their arms, legs, and other parts of their bodies.

Tattoos have many meanings

In some **cultures**, a tattoo was a sign of an important life experience. People got tattoos when they became an adult, as a reward for bravery, or as part of a religious **ceremony**.

Many modern tattoos are based on designs worn by **tribal** people in the Pacific Islands and Asia. People who wear these tattoos often simply like the design, rather than feeling connected to the original meaning.

Today most people get tattoos to express some part of their personality. They may also get a tattoo to show that they are a member of a group, or to show their connection to a culture.

How tattoos work

Tattoos are made by using needles to **inject** dyes under the skin, into the layer of flesh called the dermis. Because the dyes are injected beneath the skin, the pattern does not fade as the top layer of skin wears away. A modern tattoo machine can drive needles into the skin up to 3,000 times a minute!

Tattoo artists

Skilled tattoo artists may train with a teacher for five years or more before they are ready to tattoo on their own. Tattoo designs can take hours to complete. Tattoo artists protect their customers by working in **sanitary** (clean) conditions.

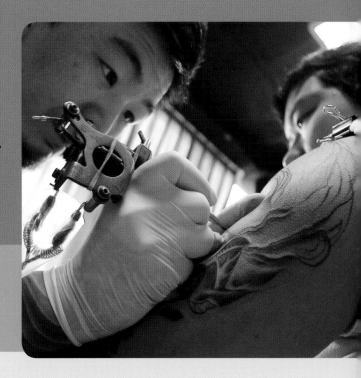

Not only do tattoo artists create art – they do it on living skin!

Piercing

During **piercing** a hole is made in the body with a needle. Then a piece of jewellery is put through the hole. After the hole heals, it is easy to take the jewellery out and put it back in. Rings and rods are the most common jewellery used.

Many piercings, many reasons

Many **cultures** practise body piercing. Ears and noses are pierced most often. In some cultures, piercings have special meaning. For example, in India infants have their ears pierced as part of a religious **ceremony**.

In Europe during the 1500s, both men and women wore earrings. By the 1900s, earrings were mostly worn by women. In Western countries, men mostly wore earrings to be rebellious. Today, it is fairly common among both women and men.

The playwright William Shakespeare (1564–1616) had his ears pierced, as did many other men of his day.

Piercings everywhere

The most common body part to get pierced is the ear. Instead of just piercing earlobes, people now put piercings through many different parts of their ears.

Pierced noses, lips, and even tongues have followed as areas to be pierced. "Surface piercings" go through any loose piece of skin, such as the eyebrow.

"Stretching" has also become popular in recent years. People place wide rods, called plugs, through their piercings. Over time, they stretch the holes with larger and larger plugs. Once stretched, these holes will never close up.

Too many?

Elaine Davidson of Scotland holds the title of the Most Pierced Woman in the World. She has more than 6,000 piercings.

Some people stretch their piercings using large plugs.

The other side of body art

Many people do not like body art. They may think someone who has many **tattoos** and **piercings** is immature and cannot be trusted. Some people link piercings and tattoos with criminal activity.

Workplace problems

Many companies will not hire people who have piercings and tattoos. They may allow women to wear earrings, but only in their earlobes. Men may not be allowed to wear any piercings. Both men and women may need to cover their tattoos. Some jobs require men and women to remove jewellery worn in piercings because of safety concerns.

Many schools also have rules about the kinds of piercing and tattoos students may wear. These attitudes are changing, but not quickly.

Some people may find this man's tattoos and piercings threatening.

Dangers of piercing

Body piercing can create some health risks. Some people have **allergic** reactions to products used to clean the piercing, or even to the metal in the jewellery. **Infections** can occur during the piercing or healing process, especially if the conditions are not **sanitary**. Lip piercings can injure the gums underneath. Because of these risks, people should only get piercings from qualified professionals.

A pierced ear can take weeks to heal. During this time, it is important to keep the piercing clean.

Removing tattoos

Almost 20 per cent of people who get tattoos change their mind later in life. Tattoos can be removed using lasers. It usually takes many sessions and can be very painful. Even then, complete removal is not guaranteed.

Looking to the future

Science and design are working together to create new kinds of body art. Some of these methods are **temporary**, while others involve surgery.

Body implants

An extreme form of body art places **implants** under the skin. In some cases, the skin heals over the implants, leaving raised patterns in the skin. Other times, spikes, horns, or other ornaments are attached to the implants.

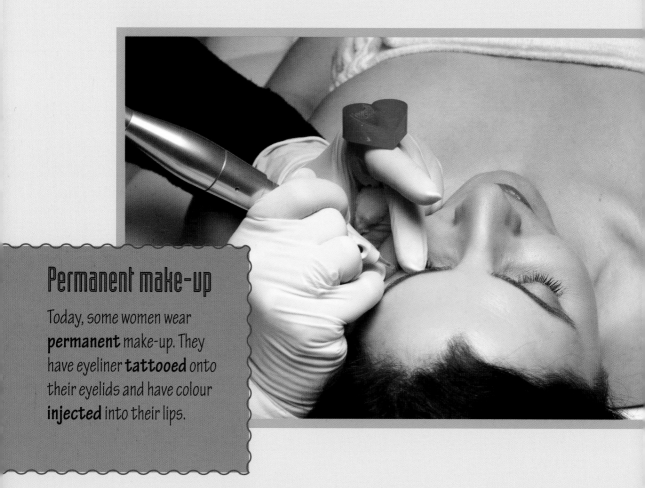

Permanent make-up

Today, some women wear **permanent** make-up. They have eyeliner **tattooed** onto their eyelids and have colour **injected** into their lips.

What next?

The future of body art is impossible to predict. Plastic surgery, in which people alter their physical appearance, is common. In 2010 a team of surgeons in Spain successfully performed the first full face transplant. This was done to repair damage from an accident, but it opens the door to new possibilities. Scientists are also currently experimenting with ways to tint eyes and skin.

Since the beginning of time, human beings have decorated their bodies. This is not likely to change. Only time will tell what kinds of body decoration will come with new technologies.

The future

In the future, people may reshape their bodies in many ways. One woman had her ears reshaped by a doctor. Implants under her skin created a new ridge above her eyes. Fat injected into her lips made them larger and fuller. Her skin and eyes have been tinted new colours. She also has tattoos that make her look like she has scales.

Glossary

allergic becoming sick or getting a rash from something

blusher red make-up used on the cheeks

camouflage colouring that allows something to blend in with the background. A tiger's stripes are a natural form of camouflage.

ceremony formal event that has meaning for people. A graduation is a ceremony students are happy to go through.

culture group of people who share a common background, traditions, and way of life. Every country has its own culture.

dung solid waste created by an animal. An elephant produces a lot of dung.

implant object that is placed under the skin. Some people have implants added to their bodies as a form of body art.

infection disease caused by germs

inject put something under the skin

Kabuki classical Japanese musical drama. Kabuki plays are not realistic and sometimes last for several hours.

Kathakali traditional play with music and dance performed in India

Maori native people of New Zealand

mehndi method of painting designs on hands and feet. Mehndi was originally used to paint a bride before her wedding.

moko permanent face and body marks worn by Maori people

permanent lasting forever. Tattoos are made with permanent ink.

pierce make a hole in something. When you get your ear pierced, a needle is pushed through your earlobe.

sanitary clean and free from germs

soot ash that's left after a fire

tattoo design that is inked into the skin. The word is also used to describe the act of creating this design in the skin.

temporary lasting for a short time. Temporary tattoos wash off after a short time.

tribal people, art, or activities belonging to a group of people that live together

tribe organized group of people who live together and share beliefs and activities

Find out more

Books

Face Painting, Caro Childs and Chris Cauldron (Usborne Publishing, 2007)

Tattoos and Indigenous Peoples, Judith Levin (Rosen, 2008)

Websites

Young people's health
kidshealth.org/kid/girlstuff/pierced_ears.html/
This US website provides information on looking after your ears if you get them pierced.

Face painting designs
www.facepaintingdesigns.co.uk
This site has ideas for face painting designs and where to buy face paints from.

History of cosmetics
www.rpsgb.org.uk/informationresources/museum/exhibitions/exhibition04/
musex04histcosm.html
Learn more about the history of cosmetics on this web page.

Place to visit

Museum of London
150 London Wall
London EC2Y 5HN
www.museumoflondon.org.uk
The Museum of London has an extensive collection of cosmetics and advertising from the early 1900s to today.

Index